90-DAY

Gratitude
Journal

Thankfulness Each Day
Will Transform Your Life!

Bento C. Leal III

Belongs to:

_____

90-DAY GRATITUDE JOURNAL

ISBN: 978-0-578-86063-3

Cover by Zakarianada
Interior flourish and floral clip art by FreshCutsStudio

Disclaimer:
This book is for entertainment purposes only. The views expressed are those of the author alone and should not be taken as expert advice. Although the author and publisher have made every effort to ensure that the information in this book was correct at press time, the author and publisher do not assume and hereby disclaim any liability to any party for any loss, damage, or disruption caused by errors or omissions, whether such errors or omissions result from negligence, accident, or any other cause.

Dear Reader,

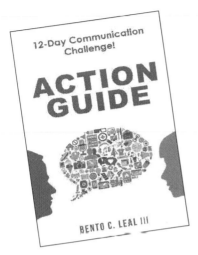

As a

Thank You

for getting this
90-Day Gratitude Journal
I am happy to give
you as a

FREE GIFT

this downloadable and printable
version of the

12-DAY
COMMUNICATION CHALLENGE!
ACTION GUIDE

This Action Guide will help you put into practice the key
communication skills of empathic listening, speaking, and
dialogue to create healthy, successful relationships
at home, work—anywhere!

Go to this link to
download your Free Gift!

www.bentoleal.com/gratitude

*Try This Communication Challenge
To Create Relationships You Will Truly
Be Grateful For!*

> ## Congratulations!
> *You have the 90-Day Gratitude Journal in your hands!*
> *My hope is that writing in this journal will benefit*
> *you greatly in all aspects of your life!*

PURPOSE OF THIS JOURNAL

This Gratitude Journal is designed for two purposes: 1) to help you reflect on and write down each day who and what you are grateful for— the people, circumstances, events, and even challenges and difficulties, and 2) by doing so, cultivate within yourself a growing and ever-deepening attitude of Gratitude that will carry forward throughout your life.

GRATITUDE DEFINITION

What is Gratitude? There are several definitions, some long and some short. This one from Oxford Languages is my favorite: **"Gratitude: noun, the quality of being thankful; readiness to show appreciation for and to return kindness."** Gratitude is an emotion that is both felt within oneself and expressed without.

WHY GRATITUDE?

Why is being grateful so important? **Simply, having an attitude of gratitude—thankfulness—makes for a healthier, happier, more fulfilling life.** It helps you become more appreciative for whoever and whatever comes your way. You will also be more equipped to maintain a positive outlook on life enabling you to go through life's ups and downs with greater confidence, ease, and peace of mind.

Ralph Waldo Emerson once said, "Cultivate the habit of being grateful for every good thing that comes to you, and to give thanks continuously...(and) because all things have contributed to your advancement, you should include all things in your gratitude."

You may not have control over many of the events that take place in your life, but you *do* have control over your attitude and responses to them. Gratitude is a positive state of mind that puts you in control of how you see and experience life.

BENEFITS OF GRATITUDE

Studies* have shown that developing and maintaining a grateful attitude has many immediate and long-term benefits:

- **Improved Mental and Physical Health** – less anxiety, less stress, longer life
- **Peace of Mind** – greater sense of calmness and stability
- **Greater Happiness** – more satisfaction, more joy
- **Better Relationships** – greater empathy, appreciation, closeness
- **Increased Marital Satisfaction** – greater feelings of contentment, commitment, and stability, especially during difficult times
- **Inner Strength** – greater resilience in dealing with life's challenges
- **Hopefulness** – optimism about the future and expectations of success
- **Self-Confidence** – greater control of your thoughts, feelings, and actions

See studies and findings of the above-mentioned benefits in the articles listed under Gratitude Resources at the end of this journal on page 121.

WHY 90 DAYS?

90 days is a solid amount of time to start developing the habit of journaling who and what you are grateful for. Think of it as a 90-day training period to build your attitude of gratitude. As the days become weeks, the process will ultimately become a welcome routine, something you look forward to, a normal part of your day and life, and something you'll want to continue doing long after the 90 days are over.

Also, if you miss a day or two for whatever reason, don't worry, just get back into rhythm by resuming writing in your journal the next day. Think of it as building a "gratitude muscle"—the more you exercise it, the stronger and more durable it becomes. Keep in mind that your goal is not simply to jot down events and close the book, but to use that reflective writing time to develop a lifestyle of heartfelt gratitude that positively affects every aspect of your life.

HOW TO USE THIS JOURNAL

This 90-day journal is divided into 10-day segments—one page for each day—followed by a couple of review pages at the end of each 10-day segment.

1) **At the end of each day, review in your mind what transpired in the day**—the people you interacted with, the events, situations, problems, etc. As you review them, think of what you appreciate about them. <u>Try to calm your mind and not rush this process.</u> The more time you spend on reflection and writing, the more this writing experience will become a special and important part of your day and life.

2) **As you reflect, consider not only what occurred that particular day, but other thoughts that come to mind**, such as, "I'm grateful for being alive!" or "I'm grateful for my high school coach" even though that may be many years in the past, or "I'm grateful for gravity!" Anything is okay, after all, it's *YOUR* gratitude journal, and the more people and things you are grateful for, the better for developing your attitude of gratitude.

3) **If you're stuck with how to articulate how you feel, use the table of words at the bottom of the pages to help you recall people and events.**

4) **Write one or more entries of gratitude—short or long—each day.** The more entries you write, the better. If you can, strive to identify 7 or more instances of gratitude each day. This will encourage you to go beyond the immediately recognizable and to stretch your recall more deeply about instances present and past. Again, use this time to stretch and grow your "gratitude muscle".

5) **Read the inspirational quotes each day.** They can add perspective and encourage you as you proceed on this gratitude journey. If you enjoy inspirational quotes on gratitude from other sources, such as self-help resources, faith or spiritual books, holy scriptures, etc., read those as well. These resources have the power to build up your mind and heart of gratitude.

6) **Commit to do the above process for 10 days straight.** Pick the time of day to do it that works best for you and be consistent.

7) **On the 10th day, take some extra time to write in the 2 review pages and have fun doing a drawing as well.** These pages give you a chance to pause, reflect, and recap what you've written the previous 10 days and track how you've grown in gratitude. Spending a few moments drawing a picture is another powerful and enjoyable way of feeling and expressing your gratitude.

8) **Then start on the next 10 days and keep going on this process for the full 90 days.**

You can tweak the above writing process as you like. **The key is to find a daily reflection and writing routine that works best for you and stick with it.** That is how gratitude will become a habit and ultimately your underlying frame of mind.

HELPFUL TIPS

- **Build the new habit by attaching it to an existing habit.** Creating a new habit can be difficult, but it's easier when you connect it to an existing habit, such as writing in your gratitude journal after you brush your teeth before going to bed, or immediately after dinner when you're able to sit and assess your day. Then this new writing habit will "piggy-back" on that existing habit giving greater assurance that it will be done. Do what works for you.

- **Keep the journal in a convenient, visible place;** otherwise, if it's out of sight, it might be out of mind and not get done. One idea is to keep it on your sleeping pillow so that you automatically see it as you get ready for bed.

- **When you wake up in the morning, do a quick review of what you wrote the previous day.** This is a great way to jumpstart your mind on gratitude as you start your day.

- **To deepen your gratitude experience, share who and what you are grateful for to someone else**—your spouse or partner, sibling, or friend. When you voice to another person who and what you are grateful for, that helps strengthen in you what you had written in the quietness of your own mind.

BONUS TIP!

Get in the habit of saying *"Thank You"* **throughout the day—for** *ANY* **reason and** *NO* **reason!** Say it when you wake up, when you get ready to go to sleep, and often during the day—*"Thank You"*. This simple act is another great way to train your mind and heart on gratitude!

SAMPLE ENTRIES

I am Grateful for…
- Walk in the park today and seeing all the trees.
- Great conversation with (name). We haven't talked in a while.
- New project at work going well.
- My overall good health.
- My parents for raising me.
- Movie we saw tonight. Inspiring story.
- My HS swimming coach – taught me discipline and hard work.
- (Name of self-help book) – great tips for developing a positive mindset.
- Challenge I'm having with (name of co-worker) – it's teaching me patience.
- The ocean – it's beautiful and invigorating!
- My good friend (name) for always supporting me.

SOME KEY DISCOVERIES IN
GRATITUDE JOURNAL WRITING

1) **Opportunities to be grateful are everywhere!** No matter how large or small, they *ALL* have value in developing in oneself a grateful mind and heart. Be proactive—keep your eyes, ears, and mind open for people and things to be grateful for.

2) **Difficult encounters or events are also opportunities to be grateful**—seeing and appreciating the silver lining in those experiences for lessons learned and how they are helping you grow your heart of patience and understanding through them.

3) **Write as many or as few points of gratitude each day as you like. Writing 7 to 10 points is a good exercise**—sometimes it's easy to come up with that many points of gratitude, and other times you may have to stretch your thinking to get that many. But again, there are always things to be grateful for, even the seemingly mundane or insignificant things you might normally overlook and take for granted. Those can be special too.

4) **Expressing gratitude to someone takes it from being an inner feeling to a substantial act.** When a person has said or done something you are grateful for, tell them. Give them the gift of appreciation. They will appreciate being appreciated.

5) **Developing an attitude of gratitude is a life-long journey and not a short-term endeavor.** It's about mindfully developing and keeping a grateful perspective throughout each day and continuing that perspective day after day. It's not easy to maintain that perspective consistently but making the effort to do so is how one grows an overall attitude of gratitude.

LETTER TO SELF

Writing a letter to yourself is an excellent way to strengthen your commitment to the overall purpose of this journal, which is to instill an attitude of gratitude into your life.

Dear _____,
          Your Name

You are now embarking on a 90-day journey to develop a grateful heart and mind—an attitude of gratitude—to be thankful for all the people and situations that come your way.

Set your mind on gratitude. Think of both the small and big things you can be grateful for.

There will be ups and downs along the way but try to see the positives even in the people and circumstances that challenge you. That is how you will grow.

Keep your chin up and enjoy the ride. I believe in you!

Signed,
Your deeper self,

_____   _____
          Your Name   *Date*

Enjoy Your 90-Day Gratitude Journey!

Day 1

Day:_____ Date:____/____/_____

Today I am Grateful for...

1. _____

2. _____

3. _____

4. _____

5. _____

6. _____

7. _____

8. _____

9. _____

10. _____

The words below may prompt your recollection of who and what you are grateful for and why:

Spouse / Partner	Parent / Child / Sibling	Teacher / Friend
Colleague / Co-Worker	Conversation	Meeting / Gathering
Spirituality / Faith / Belief	Reading / Study / Class	Skill / Talent / Ability
Event / Movie / Meal	Challenge / Problem	Opportunity
Accomplishment	Insight / Discovery	Project / Work
Lesson Learned	Help / Assistance	Purchase / Sale
Inspiration	Compliment	Breakthrough
Trip / Outing	Gift / Benefit	Pet / Nature

Day 2

Day:_____ Date:_____/_____/_____

Today I am Grateful for…

1. _____

2. _____

3. _____

4. _____

5. _____

6. _____

7. _____

8. _____

9. _____

10. _____

Daily Reflection:
*"I am grateful for these people and experiences in my life!
They are helping me grow into a stronger, better,
and more successful person! Thank you!"*

*"At times, our own light goes out and is rekindled by a spark from
another person. Each of us has cause to think with deep gratitude
of those who have lighted the flame within us."*

~ Albert Schweitzer

Day 3

Today I am Grateful for…

1. _____
2. _____
3. _____
4. _____
5. _____
6. _____
7. _____
8. _____
9. _____
10. _____

The words below may prompt your recollection
of <u>who</u> you are grateful for and why:

Spouse	Partner	Parent
Child	Sibling	Grandparent
Relative	Teacher / Pastor	Mentor / Coach
Friend	Colleague	Co-Worker
Customer	Neighbor	Stranger

Day 4

Day:_____ Date:_____/_____/_____

Today I am Grateful for...

1. _____

2. _____

3. _____

4. _____

5. _____

6. _____

7. _____

8. _____

9. _____

10. _____

I am happiest when...

_____

because _____

_____

_____

*"I don't have to chase extraordinary moments to find happiness—
it's right in front of me if I'm paying attention
and practicing gratitude."*

~ Brené Brown

Day 5

Day:_____ Date:_____/_____/_____

Today I am Grateful for...

1. _____

2. _____

3. _____

4. _____

5. _____

6. _____

7. _____

8. _____

9. _____

10. _____

The words below may prompt your recollection
of <u>what</u> you are grateful for and why:

Spirituality / Faith / Belief	Help / Assistance	Skill / Talent / Ability
Movie / Show	Meal / Food	Housing / Shelter
Purchase / Sale	Letter / Message	Book / Article
Pet	Nature	Class / Course
Art / Music	Job / Career	Health

Day 6

Day:_____ Date:_____/_____/_____

Today I am Grateful for...

1. _____

2. _____

3. _____

4. _____

5. _____

6. _____

7. _____

8. _____

9. _____

10. _____

My favorite time of year is...

_____

because _____

_____

_____

"What you truly acknowledge truly is yours. Invite your heart to be grateful and your 'thank you's' will be heard even when you don't use words."

~ Pavithra Mehta

Day 7

Day:_____ Date:_____/_____/_____

Today I am Grateful for...

1. _____

2. _____

3. _____

4. _____

5. _____

6. _____

7. _____

8. _____

9. _____

10. _____

The words below may prompt your recollection
of <u>experiences</u> you are grateful for and why:

Conversation	Meeting / Gathering	Trip / Outing
Accomplishment	Insight / Discovery	Work Project
Challenge / Problem	Lesson Learned	Opportunity
Inspiration	Compliment	Breakthrough
Giving a Gift	Receiving a Gift	Benefit Received

Day 8

Day:_____ Date:_____/_____/_____

Today I am Grateful for...

1. _____

2. _____

3. _____

4. _____

5. _____

6. _____

7. _____

8. _____

9. _____

10. _____

A person I greatly admire is...

_____   _____

because _____

_____

_____

> *"'Thank you' is the best prayer that anyone could say.*
> *I say that one a lot. Thank you expresses extreme*
> *gratitude, humility, understanding."*
>
> *~ Alice Walker*

Day 9

Today I am Grateful for…

1. _____

2. _____

3. _____

4. _____

5. _____

6. _____

7. _____

8. _____

9. _____

10. _____

The words below may prompt your recollection
of <u>activities</u> you are grateful for and why:

Reading / Studying	Teaching / Learning	Exercise / Yoga
Praying / Meditating	Biking / Swimming	Walking / Jogging
Writing / Creating	Building	Fixing / Repairing
Volunteering / Donating	Cooking / Cleaning	Helping / Assisting

Day 10

Day:_____ Date:____/____/_____

Today I am Grateful for…

1. _____

2. _____

3. _____

4. _____

5. _____

6. _____

7. _____

8. _____

9. _____

10. _____

A skill or talent I have that most people don't know I have is…

_____

I'm grateful for this ability because _____

_____

_____

> *"The discipline of gratitude is the explicit effort to acknowledge*
> *that all I am and have is given to me as a gift of love,*
> *a gift to be celebrated with joy."*
>
> *~ Henri Nouwen*

Pause & Review

As I review my entries of the past 10 days, these are the experiences of Gratitude that were most meaningful to me and why...

1. _____

    _____

2. _____

    _____

3. _____

    _____

4. _____

    _____

Express Your Gratitude

*As I reflect on my life, including recent events,
these are people I will express Gratitude to right away:*

Name	Reason to Thank Them	What I Will Do

Schedule and follow through on your actions to thank them
(e.g., conversation, phone call, text, email, card, gift, meal, etc.).
They will appreciate being appreciated!

Draw Someone or Something You're Grateful For!

Personal Check-In

*How is this daily practice of Gratitude
improving my life, circumstances, and relationships?
And how do I feel about these developments?*

_____

_____

_____

_____

_____

_____

_____

Have a Grateful Next 10 days!

Day 11

Day:_____ Date:_____/_____/_____

Today I am Grateful for...

1. _____

2. _____

3. _____

4. _____

5. _____

6. _____

7. _____

8. _____

9. _____

10. _____

The words below may prompt your recollection
of who and what you are grateful for and why:

Spouse / Partner	Parent / Child / Sibling	Teacher / Friend
Colleague / Co-Worker	Conversation	Meeting / Gathering
Spirituality / Faith / Belief	Reading / Study / Class	Skill / Talent / Ability
Event / Movie / Meal	Challenge / Problem	Opportunity
Accomplishment	Insight / Discovery	Project / Work
Lesson Learned	Help / Assistance	Purchase / Sale
Inspiration	Compliment	Breakthrough
Trip / Outing	Gift / Benefit	Pet / Nature

Day 12

Day:_____ Date:_____/_____/_____

Today I am Grateful for...

1. _____

2. _____

3. _____

4. _____

5. _____

6. _____

7. _____

8. _____

9. _____

10. _____

Daily Reflection:
*"I am grateful for these people and experiences in my life!
They are helping me grow into a stronger, better,
and more successful person! Thank you!"*

*"Often people ask how I manage to be happy despite having
no arms and no legs. The quick answer is that I have a choice.
I can be angry about not having limbs, or I can be thankful
that I have a purpose. I chose gratitude."*

~ Nick Vujicic

Day 13

Today I am Grateful for...

1. _____

2. _____

3. _____

4. _____

5. _____

6. _____

7. _____

8. _____

9. _____

10. _____

The words below may prompt your recollection of <u>who</u> you are grateful for and why:

Spouse	Partner	Parent
Child	Sibling	Grandparent
Relative	Teacher / Pastor	Mentor / Coach
Friend	Colleague	Co-Worker
Customer	Neighbor	Stranger

Day 14

Day:_____ Date:_____/_____/_____

Today I am Grateful for...

1. _____

2. _____

3. _____

4. _____

5. _____

6. _____

7. _____

8. _____

9. _____

10. _____

My favorite kind of food is...

_____

_____

I love it because _____

_____

_____

"When we focus on our gratitude, the tide of disappointment goes out and the tide of love rushes in."

~ Kristin Armstrong

Day 15

Day:_____ Date:_____/_____/_____

Today I am Grateful for...

1. _____

2. _____

3. _____

4. _____

5. _____

6. _____

7. _____

8. _____

9. _____

10. _____

The words below may prompt your recollection
of <u>what</u> you are grateful for and why:

Spirituality / Faith / Belief	Help / Assistance	Skill / Talent / Ability
Movie / Show	Meal / Food	Housing / Shelter
Purchase / Sale	Letter / Message	Book / Article
Pet	Nature	Class / Course
Art / Music	Job / Career	Health

Day 16

Day:_____ Date:_____/_____/_____

Today I am Grateful for...

1. _____

2. _____

3. _____

4. _____

5. _____

6. _____

7. _____

8. _____

9. _____

10. _____

One of the greatest acts of kindness I have ever seen was...

_____

This inspired me because_____

_____

"We are constituted so that simple acts of kindness, such as giving to charity or expressing gratitude, have a positive effect on our long-term moods. The key to the happy life, it seems, is the good life: a life with sustained relationships, challenging work, and connections to community."

~ Paul Bloom

Day 17

Day:_____ Date:_____/_____/_____

Today I am Grateful for…

1. _____

2. _____

3. _____

4. _____

5. _____

6. _____

7. _____

8. _____

9. _____

10. _____

The words below may prompt your recollection
of <u>experiences</u> you are grateful for and why:

Conversation	Meeting / Gathering	Trip / Outing
Accomplishment	Insight / Discovery	Work Project
Challenge / Problem	Lesson Learned	Opportunity
Inspiration	Compliment	Breakthrough
Giving a Gift	Receiving a Gift	Benefit Received

Day 18

Day:_____ Date:_____/_____/_____

Today I am Grateful for…

1. _____

2. _____

3. _____

4. _____

5. _____

6. _____

7. _____

8. _____

9. _____

10. _____

What I love most about being in nature is…

_____

_____

_____

_____

_____

"Nature's beauty is a gift that cultivates
appreciation and gratitude."

~ Louis Schwartzberg

Day 19

Day:_____ Date:_____/_____/_____

Today I am Grateful for...

1. _____

2. _____

3. _____

4. _____

5. _____

6. _____

7. _____

8. _____

9. _____

10. _____

The words below may prompt your recollection of <u>activities</u> you are grateful for and why:

Reading / Studying	Teaching / Learning	Exercise / Yoga
Praying / Meditating	Biking / Swimming	Walking / Jogging
Writing / Creating	Building	Fixing / Repairing
Volunteering / Donating	Cooking / Cleaning	Helping / Assisting

Day 20

Day:_____ Date:_____/_____/_____

Today I am Grateful for…

1. _____

2. _____

3. _____

4. _____

5. _____

6. _____

7. _____

8. _____

9. _____

10. _____

When I'm feeling down, a positive thing I like to do to cheer me up is

_____

It makes me feel _____

_____

_____

"Gratitude is one of the strongest and most transformative states of being.
It shifts your perspective from lack to abundance and allows you
to focus on the good in your life, which in turn pulls
more goodness into your reality."

~ Jen Sincero

Pause & Review

As I review my entries of the past 10 days, these are the experiences of Gratitude that were most meaningful to me and why...

1. _____

   _____

2. _____

   _____

3. _____

   _____

4. _____

   _____

Express Your Gratitude

As I reflect on my life, including recent events, these are people I will express Gratitude to right away:

Name	Reason to Thank Them	What I Will Do

Schedule and follow through on your actions to thank them
(e.g., conversation, phone call, text, email, card, gift, meal, etc.).
They will appreciate being appreciated!

Draw Someone or Something You're Grateful For!

Personal Check-In

How is this daily practice of Gratitude
improving my life, circumstances, and relationships?
And how do I feel about these developments?

_____

_____

_____

_____

_____

_____

_____

Have a Grateful Next 10 days!

Day 21   Day:_____ Date:____/____/_____

Today I am Grateful for...

1. _____

2. _____

3. _____

4. _____

5. _____

6. _____

7. _____

8. _____

9. _____

10. _____

The words below may prompt your recollection of who and what you are grateful for and why:

Spouse / Partner	Parent / Child / Sibling	Teacher / Friend
Colleague / Co-Worker	Conversation	Meeting / Gathering
Spirituality / Faith / Belief	Reading / Study / Class	Skill / Talent / Ability
Event / Movie / Meal	Challenge / Problem	Opportunity
Accomplishment	Insight / Discovery	Project / Work
Lesson Learned	Help / Assistance	Purchase / Sale
Inspiration	Compliment	Breakthrough
Trip / Outing	Gift / Benefit	Pet / Nature

Day 22

Day:_____ Date:____/____/_____

Today I am Grateful for…

1. _____

2. _____

3. _____

4. _____

5. _____

6. _____

7. _____

8. _____

9. _____

10. _____

Daily Reflection:
"I am grateful for these people and experiences in my life!
They are helping me grow into a stronger, better,
and more successful person! Thank you!"

"The best and most beautiful things in the world
cannot be seen or even touched—
they must be felt with the heart."

~ Helen Keller

Day 23

Today I am Grateful for…

1. _____

2. _____

3. _____

4. _____

5. _____

6. _____

7. _____

8. _____

9. _____

10. _____

The words below may prompt your recollection of <u>who</u> you are grateful for and why:

Spouse	Partner	Parent
Child	Sibling	Grandparent
Relative	Teacher / Pastor	Mentor / Coach
Friend	Colleague	Co-Worker
Customer	Neighbor	Stranger

Day 24

Day:_____ Date:____/____/_____

Today I am Grateful for...

1. _____

2. _____

3. _____

4. _____

5. _____

6. _____

7. _____

8. _____

9. _____

10. _____

One of my greatest achievements in life is/was...

_____

_____

I'm proud of it because _____

_____

"Develop an attitude of gratitude, and give thanks for everything that happens to you, knowing that every step forward is a step toward achieving something bigger and better than your current situation."

~ Brian Tracy

Day 25

Day:_____ Date:_____/_____/_____

Today I am Grateful for…

1. _____

2. _____

3. _____

4. _____

5. _____

6. _____

7. _____

8. _____

9. _____

10. _____

The words below may prompt your recollection
of __what__ you are grateful for and why:

Spirituality / Faith / Belief	Help / Assistance	Skill / Talent / Ability
Movie / Show	Meal / Food	Housing / Shelter
Purchase / Sale	Letter / Message	Book / Article
Pet	Nature	Class / Course
Art / Music	Job / Career	Health

Day 26

Day:_____ Date:____/____/_____

Today I am Grateful for...

1. _____

2. _____

3. _____

4. _____

5. _____

6. _____

7. _____

8. _____

9. _____

10. _____

The teacher I learned the most from was...

_____

because _____

_____

> *"One looks back with appreciation to the brilliant teachers,*
> *but with gratitude to those who touched our human feelings.*
> *The curriculum is so much necessary raw material,*
> *but warmth is the vital element for the growing plant*
> *and for the soul of the child."*
>
> *~ Carl Jung*

Day 27

Day:_____ Date:____/____/_____

Today I am Grateful for...

1. _____

2. _____

3. _____

4. _____

5. _____

6. _____

7. _____

8. _____

9. _____

10. _____

The words below may prompt your recollection
of <u>experiences</u> you are grateful for and why:

Conversation	Meeting / Gathering	Trip / Outing
Accomplishment	Insight / Discovery	Work Project
Challenge / Problem	Lesson Learned	Opportunity
Inspiration	Compliment	Breakthrough
Giving a Gift	Receiving a Gift	Benefit Received

Day 28

Day:_____ Date:_____/_____/_____

Today I am Grateful for…

1. _____

2. _____

3. _____

4. _____

5. _____

6. _____

7. _____

8. _____

9. _____

10. _____

One of my favorite movies is…

_____

I enjoy it because _____

_____

_____

"A positive attitude is not going to save you. What it's going to do is, every day, between now and the day you die, whether that's a short time from now or a long time from now, that every day, you're going to actually live."

~ Elizabeth Edwards

Day 29

Day:_____ Date:_____/_____/_____

Today I am Grateful for…

1. _____

2. _____

3. _____

4. _____

5. _____

6. _____

7. _____

8. _____

9. _____

10. _____

The words below may prompt your recollection
of __activities__ you are grateful for and why:

Reading / Studying	Teaching / Learning	Exercise / Yoga
Praying / Meditating	Biking / Swimming	Walking / Jogging
Writing / Creating	Building	Fixing / Repairing
Volunteering / Donating	Cooking / Cleaning	Helping / Assisting

Day 30

Day:_____ Date:____/____/_____

Today I am Grateful for...

1. _____

2. _____

3. _____

4. _____

5. _____

6. _____

7. _____

8. _____

9. _____

10. _____

Five positive words (or phrases) that describe me are...

1. _____

2. _____

3. _____

4. _____

5. _____

> *"In life, one has a choice to take one of two paths:*
> *to wait for some special day–or to celebrate each special day."*
>
> *~ Rasheed Ogunlaru*

Pause & Review

As I review my entries of the past 10 days, these are the experiences of Gratitude that were most meaningful to me and why...

1. _____

   _____

2. _____

   _____

3. _____

   _____

4. _____

   _____

Express Your Gratitude

As I reflect on my life, including recent events, these are people I will express Gratitude to right away:

Name	Reason to Thank Them	What I Will Do

Schedule and follow through on your actions to thank them
(e.g., conversation, phone call, text, email, card, gift, meal, etc.).
They will appreciate being appreciated!

Draw Someone or Something You're Grateful For!

Personal Check-In

*How is this daily practice of Gratitude
improving my life, circumstances, and relationships?
And how do I feel about these developments?*

_____

_____

_____

_____

_____

_____

_____

Have a Grateful Next 10 days!

Day 31

Day:_____ Date:_____/_____/_____

Today I am Grateful for...

1. _____

2. _____

3. _____

4. _____

5. _____

6. _____

7. _____

8. _____

9. _____

10. _____

The words below may prompt your recollection
of who and what you are grateful for and why:

Spouse / Partner	Parent / Child / Sibling	Teacher / Friend
Colleague / Co-Worker	Conversation	Meeting / Gathering
Spirituality / Faith / Belief	Reading / Study / Class	Skill / Talent / Ability
Event / Movie / Meal	Challenge / Problem	Opportunity
Accomplishment	Insight / Discovery	Project / Work
Lesson Learned	Help / Assistance	Purchase / Sale
Inspiration	Compliment	Breakthrough
Trip / Outing	Gift / Benefit	Pet / Nature

Day 32

Day:_____ Date:____/____/_____

Today I am Grateful for...

1. _____

2. _____

3. _____

4. _____

5. _____

6. _____

7. _____

8. _____

9. _____

10. _____

Something I look forward to in the future is...

_____

_____

because _____

_____

_____

"You must do the things you think you cannot do."
~ Eleanor Roosevelt

Day 33

Day:_____ Date:_____/_____/_____

Today I am Grateful for…

1. _____

2. _____

3. _____

4. _____

5. _____

6. _____

7. _____

8. _____

9. _____

10. _____

The words below may prompt your recollection
of <u>who</u> you are grateful for and why:

Spouse	Partner	Parent
Child	Sibling	Grandparent
Relative	Teacher / Pastor	Mentor / Coach
Friend	Colleague	Co-Worker
Customer	Neighbor	Stranger

Day 34

Day:_____ Date:_____/_____/_____

Today I am Grateful for…

1. _____

2. _____

3. _____

4. _____

5. _____

6. _____

7. _____

8. _____

9. _____

10. _____

A song I love to hear is...

_____

*because*_____

_____

_____

"Happiness cannot be traveled to, owned, earned, worn, or consumed. Happiness is the spiritual experience of living every minute with love, grace and gratitude."

~ Denis Waitley

Day 35

Day:_____ Date:____/____/_____

Today I am Grateful for...

1. _____
2. _____
3. _____
4. _____
5. _____
6. _____
7. _____
8. _____
9. _____
10. _____

The words below may prompt your recollection of <u>what</u> you are grateful for and why:

Spirituality / Faith / Belief	Help / Assistance	Skill / Talent / Ability
Movie / Show	Meal / Food	Housing / Shelter
Purchase / Sale	Letter / Message	Book / Article
Pet	Nature	Class / Course
Art / Music	Job / Career	Health

Day 36

Day:_____ Date:____/____/_____

Today I am Grateful for...

1. _____

2. _____

3. _____

4. _____

5. _____

6. _____

7. _____

8. _____

9. _____

10. _____

An act of kindness someone did for me recently was...

_____

_____

*I felt*_____

_____

"Gratitude helps you to grow and expand; gratitude brings joy and laughter into your life and into the lives of all those around you."

~ Eileen Caddy

Day 37

Today I am Grateful for...

1. _____

2. _____

3. _____

4. _____

5. _____

6. _____

7. _____

8. _____

9. _____

10. _____

The words below may prompt your recollection
of <u>experiences</u> you are grateful for and why:

Conversation	Meeting / Gathering	Trip / Outing
Accomplishment	Insight / Discovery	Work Project
Challenge / Problem	Lesson Learned	Opportunity
Inspiration	Compliment	Breakthrough
Giving a Gift	Receiving a Gift	Benefit Received

Day 38
Day:_____ Date:____/____/_____

Today I am Grateful for...

1. _____

2. _____

3. _____

4. _____

5. _____

6. _____

7. _____

8. _____

9. _____

10. _____

The most delicious meal I ever had was...

_____

_____

*because*_____

_____

"For me... I feel like gratitude has really helped me to keep perspective on everything. The gratitude of doing what I get to do. The gratitude for my everyday life. The gratitude for simple things."

~ Joseph Benavidez

Day 39

Day:_____ Date:____/____/_____

Today I am Grateful for...

1. _____

2. _____

3. _____

4. _____

5. _____

6. _____

7. _____

8. _____

9. _____

10. _____

The words below may prompt your recollection
of <u>activities</u> you are grateful for and why:

Reading / Studying	Teaching / Learning	Exercise / Yoga
Praying / Meditating	Biking / Swimming	Walking / Jogging
Writing / Creating	Building	Fixing / Repairing
Volunteering / Donating	Cooking / Cleaning	Helping / Assisting

Day 40

Day:_____ Date:_____/_____/_____

Today I am Grateful for…

1. _____

2. _____

3. _____

4. _____

5. _____

6. _____

7. _____

8. _____

9. _____

10. _____

A challenge I'm facing that I'm determined to overcome is…

_____

_____

When I overcome it I will feel _____

_____

> *"Gratitude is the inward feeling of kindness received.*
> *Thankfulness is the natural impulse to express that feeling.*
> *Thanksgiving is the following of that impulse."*
>
> *~ Henry Van Dyke*

Pause & Review

*As I review my entries of the past 10 days, these are the experiences
of Gratitude that were most meaningful to me and why...*

1. _____

_____

2. _____

_____

3. _____

_____

4. _____

_____

Express Your Gratitude

*As I reflect on my life, including recent events,
these are people I will express Gratitude to right away:*

Name	Reason to Thank Them	What I Will Do

Schedule and follow through on your actions to thank them
(e.g., conversation, phone call, text, email, card, gift, meal, etc.).
They will appreciate being appreciated!

Draw Someone or Something You're Grateful For!

Personal Check-In

*How is this daily practice of Gratitude
improving my life, circumstances, and relationships?
And how do I feel about these developments?*

_____

_____

_____

_____

_____

_____

Have a Grateful Next 10 days!

Day 41

Day:_____ Date:_____/_____/_____

Today I am Grateful for...

1. _____

2. _____

3. _____

4. _____

5. _____

6. _____

7. _____

8. _____

9. _____

10. _____

The words below may prompt your recollection
of who and what you are grateful for and why:

Spouse / Partner	Parent / Child / Sibling	Teacher / Friend
Colleague / Co-Worker	Conversation	Meeting / Gathering
Spirituality / Faith / Belief	Reading / Study / Class	Skill / Talent / Ability
Event / Movie / Meal	Challenge / Problem	Opportunity
Accomplishment	Insight / Discovery	Project / Work
Lesson Learned	Help / Assistance	Purchase / Sale
Inspiration	Compliment	Breakthrough
Trip / Outing	Gift / Benefit	Pet / Nature

Day 42

Day:_____ Date:_____/_____/_____

Today I am Grateful for…

1. _____

2. _____

3. _____

4. _____

5. _____

6. _____

7. _____

8. _____

9. _____

10. _____

One of my favorite heroes in history is…

_____

What I appreciate about him/her is…

_____

_____

_____

> *"Gratitude is not only the greatest of virtues,*
> *but the parent of all the others."*
>
> *~ Marcus Tullius Cicero*

Day 43

Today I am Grateful for...

1. _____

2. _____

3. _____

4. _____

5. _____

6. _____

7. _____

8. _____

9. _____

10. _____

The words below may prompt your recollection of <u>who</u> you are grateful for and why:

Spouse	Partner	Parent
Child	Sibling	Grandparent
Relative	Teacher / Pastor	Mentor / Coach
Friend	Colleague	Co-Worker
Customer	Neighbor	Stranger

Day 44

Day:_____ Date:____/____/_____

Today I am Grateful for...

1. _____

2. _____

3. _____

4. _____

5. _____

6. _____

7. _____

8. _____

9. _____

10. _____

A relationship I'm especially grateful for is...

_____

_____

*because*_____

_____

_____

"When you view your world with an attitude of gratitude,
you are training yourself to focus on the good in life."

~ Paul J. Meyer

Day 45

Day:_____ Date:____/____/_____

Today I am Grateful for…

1. _____

2. _____

3. _____

4. _____

5. _____

6. _____

7. _____

8. _____

9. _____

10. _____

The words below may prompt your recollection
of <u>what</u> you are grateful for and why:

Spirituality / Faith / Belief	Help / Assistance	Skill / Talent / Ability
Movie / Show	Meal / Food	Housing / Shelter
Purchase / Sale	Letter / Message	Book / Article
Pet	Nature	Class / Course
Art / Music	Job / Career	Health

Day 46

Day:_____ Date:_____/_____/_____

Today I am Grateful for…

1. _____

2. _____

3. _____

4. _____

5. _____

6. _____

7. _____

8. _____

9. _____

10. _____

One of my favorite childhood memories was…

_____

_____

*I felt*_____

_____

_____

"Gratitude makes sense of our past, brings peace for today, and creates a vision for tomorrow."

~ Melody Beattie

Day 47　　Day:_____ Date:____/____/_____

Today I am Grateful for…

1. _____

2. _____

3. _____

4. _____

5. _____

6. _____

7. _____

8. _____

9. _____

10. _____

The words below may prompt your recollection
of <u>experiences</u> you are grateful for and why:

Conversation	Meeting / Gathering	Trip / Outing
Accomplishment	Insight / Discovery	Work Project
Challenge / Problem	Lesson Learned	Opportunity
Inspiration	Compliment	Breakthrough
Giving a Gift	Receiving a Gift	Benefit Received

Day 48

Day:_____ Date:_____/_____/_____

Today I am Grateful for...

1. _____

2. _____

3. _____

4. _____

5. _____

6. _____

7. _____

8. _____

9. _____

10. _____

A key breakthrough I had in my life was...

_____

_____

*What I learned from that was*_____

_____

_____

"Never lose the childlike wonder. Show gratitude...
Don't complain; just work harder... Never give up."

~ Randy Pausch

Day 49

Today I am Grateful for...

1. _____

2. _____

3. _____

4. _____

5. _____

6. _____

7. _____

8. _____

9. _____

10. _____

The words below may prompt your recollection
of <u>activities</u> you are grateful for and why:

Reading / Studying	Teaching / Learning	Exercise / Yoga
Praying / Meditating	Biking / Swimming	Walking / Jogging
Writing / Creating	Building	Fixing / Repairing
Volunteering / Donating	Cooking / Cleaning	Helping / Assisting

Day 50

Day:_____ Date:____/____/_____

Today I am Grateful for...

1. _____

2. _____

3. _____

4. _____

5. _____

6. _____

7. _____

8. _____

9. _____

10. _____

My favorite subjects in school were...

_____

_____

I enjoyed them because _____

_____

_____

"Feeling gratitude isn't born in us – it's something we are taught, and in turn, we teach our children."

~ Joyce Brothers

Pause & Review

As I review my entries of the past 10 days, these are the experiences of Gratitude that were most meaningful to me and why...

1. _____

   _____

2. _____

   _____

3. _____

   _____

4. _____

   _____

Express Your Gratitude

As I reflect on my life, including recent events,
these are people I will express Gratitude to right away:

Name	Reason to Thank Them	What I Will Do

Schedule and follow through on your actions to thank them
(e.g., conversation, phone call, text, email, card, gift, meal, etc.).
They will appreciate being appreciated!

Draw Someone or Something You're Grateful For!

Personal Check-In

*How is this daily practice of Gratitude
improving my life, circumstances, and relationships?
And how do I feel about these developments?*

_____

_____

_____

_____

_____

_____

Have a Grateful Next 10 days!

Day 51

Day:_____ Date:_____/_____/_____

Today I am Grateful for...

1. _____

2. _____

3. _____

4. _____

5. _____

6. _____

7. _____

8. _____

9. _____

10. _____

The words below may prompt your recollection
of who and what you are grateful for and why:

Spouse / Partner	Parent / Child / Sibling	Teacher / Friend
Colleague / Co-Worker	Conversation	Meeting / Gathering
Spirituality / Faith / Belief	Reading / Study / Class	Skill / Talent / Ability
Event / Movie / Meal	Challenge / Problem	Opportunity
Accomplishment	Insight / Discovery	Project / Work
Lesson Learned	Help / Assistance	Purchase / Sale
Inspiration	Compliment	Breakthrough
Trip / Outing	Gift / Benefit	Pet / Nature

Day 52

Day:_____ Date:____/____/_____

Today I am Grateful for...

1. _____

2. _____

3. _____

4. _____

5. _____

6. _____

7. _____

8. _____

9. _____

10. _____

An act of kindness or generosity I did recently was...

_____

_____

I felt _____

_____

> *"No one who achieves success does so without acknowledging the help of others. The wise and confident acknowledge this help with gratitude."*
>
> *~ Alfred North Whitehead*

Day 53

Today I am Grateful for…

1. _____

2. _____

3. _____

4. _____

5. _____

6. _____

7. _____

8. _____

9. _____

10. _____

The words below may prompt your recollection of <u>who</u> you are grateful for and why:

Spouse	Partner	Parent
Child	Sibling	Grandparent
Relative	Teacher / Pastor	Mentor / Coach
Friend	Colleague	Co-Worker
Customer	Neighbor	Stranger

Day 54

Day:_____ Date:_____/_____/_____

Today I am Grateful for…

1. _____

2. _____

3. _____

4. _____

5. _____

6. _____

7. _____

8. _____

9. _____

10. _____

One of the best books I ever read was…

_____

*I enjoyed it because*_____

_____

_____

_____

"Be thankful for the small things.
It is in them that your strength lies."

~ Mother Theresa

Day 55   Day:_____ Date:____/____/_____

Today I am Grateful for...

1. _____

2. _____

3. _____

4. _____

5. _____

6. _____

7. _____

8. _____

9. _____

10. _____

The words below may prompt your recollection
of <u>what</u> you are grateful for and why:

Spirituality / Faith / Belief	Help / Assistance	Skill / Talent / Ability
Movie / Show	Meal / Food	Housing / Shelter
Purchase / Sale	Letter / Message	Book / Article
Pet	Nature	Class / Course
Art / Music	Job / Career	Health

Day 56

Day:_____ Date:_____/_____/_____

Today I am Grateful for…

1. _____

2. _____

3. _____

4. _____

5. _____

6. _____

7. _____

8. _____

9. _____

10. _____

A goal on my bucket list that keeps me going is…

_____

_____

*This goal inspires me because*_____

_____

> *"The key to life is your attitude. Whether you're single or married or have kids or don't have kids, it's how you look at your life, what you make of it. It's about making the best of your life wherever you are in life."*
>
> *~ Candace Bushnell*

Day 57   Day:_____ Date:_____/_____/_____

Today I am Grateful for...

1. _____

2. _____

3. _____

4. _____

5. _____

6. _____

7. _____

8. _____

9. _____

10. _____

The words below may prompt your recollection of <u>experiences</u> you are grateful for and why:

Conversation	Meeting / Gathering	Trip / Outing
Accomplishment	Insight / Discovery	Work Project
Challenge / Problem	Lesson Learned	Opportunity
Inspiration	Compliment	Breakthrough
Giving a Gift	Receiving a Gift	Benefit Received

Day 58

Day:_____ Date:_____/_____/_____

Today I am Grateful for...

1. _____

2. _____

3. _____

4. _____

5. _____

6. _____

7. _____

8. _____

9. _____

10. _____

When I think of all the animals, one that really impresses me is...

_____

*because*_____

_____

"Give yourself a gift of five minutes of contemplation in awe of everything you see around you. Go outside and turn your attention to the many miracles around you. This five-minute-a-day regimen of appreciation and gratitude will help you to focus your life in awe."

~ Wayne Dyer

Day 59

Day:_____ Date:_____/_____/_____

Today I am Grateful for…

1. _____

2. _____

3. _____

4. _____

5. _____

6. _____

7. _____

8. _____

9. _____

10. _____

The words below may prompt your recollection
of <u>activities</u> you are grateful for and why:

Reading / Studying	Teaching / Learning	Exercise / Yoga
Praying / Meditating	Biking / Swimming	Walking / Jogging
Writing / Creating	Building	Fixing / Repairing
Volunteering / Donating	Cooking / Cleaning	Helping / Assisting

Day 60

Day:_____ Date:_____/_____/_____

Today I am Grateful for...

1. _____

2. _____

3. _____

4. _____

5. _____

6. _____

7. _____

8. _____

9. _____

10. _____

A positive story I read, heard, or saw in the news recently was...

_____

_____

*I liked it because*_____

_____

_____

> *"A strong positive mental attitude will create*
> *more miracles than any wonder drug."*
>
> *~ Patricia Neal*

Pause & Review

As I review my entries of the past 10 days, these are the experiences of Gratitude that were most meaningful to me and why...

1. _____

   _____

2. _____

   _____

3. _____

   _____

4. _____

   _____

Express Your Gratitude

As I reflect on my life, including recent events,
these are people I will express Gratitude to right away:

Name	Reason to Thank Them	What I Will Do

Schedule and follow through on your actions to thank them
(e.g., conversation, phone call, text, email, card, gift, meal, etc.).
They will appreciate being appreciated!

Draw Someone or Something You're Grateful For!

Personal Check-In

*How is this daily practice of Gratitude
improving my life, circumstances, and relationships?
And how do I feel about these developments?*

_____

_____

_____

_____

_____

_____

Have a Grateful Next 10 days!

Day 61

Day:_____ Date:____/____/_____

Today I am Grateful for...

1. _____

2. _____

3. _____

4. _____

5. _____

6. _____

7. _____

8. _____

9. _____

10. _____

The words below may prompt your recollection
of who and what you are grateful for and why:

Spouse / Partner	Parent / Child / Sibling	Teacher / Friend
Colleague / Co-Worker	Conversation	Meeting / Gathering
Spirituality / Faith / Belief	Reading / Study / Class	Skill / Talent / Ability
Event / Movie / Meal	Challenge / Problem	Opportunity
Accomplishment	Insight / Discovery	Project / Work
Lesson Learned	Help / Assistance	Purchase / Sale
Inspiration	Compliment	Breakthrough
Trip / Outing	Gift / Benefit	Pet / Nature

Day 62

Day:_____ Date:____/____/_____

Today I am Grateful for...

1. _____

2. _____

3. _____

4. _____

5. _____

6. _____

7. _____

8. _____

9. _____

10. _____

One of my favorite games as a child was...

_____

*I really enjoyed it because*_____

_____

_____

"It's wonderful to be grateful. To have that gratitude well out from deep within you and pour out in waves. Once you truly experience this, you will never want to give it up."

~ Srikumar Rao

Day 63

Today I am Grateful for...

1. _____

2. _____

3. _____

4. _____

5. _____

6. _____

7. _____

8. _____

9. _____

10. _____

The words below may prompt your recollection
of <u>who</u> you are grateful for and why:

Spouse	Partner	Parent
Child	Sibling	Grandparent
Relative	Teacher / Pastor	Mentor / Coach
Friend	Colleague	Co-Worker
Customer	Neighbor	Stranger

Day 64

Day:_____ Date:_____/_____/_____

Today I am Grateful for...

1. _____

2. _____

3. _____

4. _____

5. _____

6. _____

7. _____

8. _____

9. _____

10. _____

A big challenge I faced and overcame was...

_____

_____

What I learned from that experience was...

_____

_____

_____

"Gratitude changes the pangs of memory into a tranquil joy."
~ Dietrich Bonhoeffer

Day 65

Today I am Grateful for...

1. _____

2. _____

3. _____

4. _____

5. _____

6. _____

7. _____

8. _____

9. _____

10. _____

**The words below may prompt your recollection
of <u>what</u> you are grateful for and why:**

Spirituality / Faith / Belief	Help / Assistance	Skill / Talent / Ability
Movie / Show	Meal / Food	Housing / Shelter
Purchase / Sale	Letter / Message	Book / Article
Pet	Nature	Class / Course
Art / Music	Job / Career	Health

Day 66

Day:_____ Date:_____/_____/_____

Today I am Grateful for...

1. _____

2. _____

3. _____

4. _____

5. _____

6. _____

7. _____

8. _____

9. _____

10. _____

When I go for a brisk walk outside, I feel...

_____

_____

*I enjoy doing exercise because*_____

_____

_____

> *"Have gratitude for all that you have,*
> *and you can be happy exactly as you are."*
>
> *~ Mandy Ingber*

Day 67 Day:_____ Date:____/____/_____

Today I am Grateful for…

1. _____
2. _____
3. _____
4. _____
5. _____
6. _____
7. _____
8. _____
9. _____
10. _____

The words below may prompt your recollection
of <u>experiences</u> you are grateful for and why:

Conversation	Meeting / Gathering	Trip / Outing
Accomplishment	Insight / Discovery	Work Project
Challenge / Problem	Lesson Learned	Opportunity
Inspiration	Compliment	Breakthrough
Giving a Gift	Receiving a Gift	Benefit Received

Day 68

Day:_____ Date:____/____/_____

Today I am Grateful for...

1. _____

2. _____

3. _____

4. _____

5. _____

6. _____

7. _____

8. _____

9. _____

10. _____

Aspects of my physical health I'm grateful for are...

_____

_____

_____

_____

"Gratitude is the healthiest of all human emotions. The more you express gratitude for what you have, the more likely you will have even more to express gratitude for."

~ Zig Ziglar

Day 69

Day:_____ Date:_____/_____/_____

Today I am Grateful for...

1. _____

2. _____

3. _____

4. _____

5. _____

6. _____

7. _____

8. _____

9. _____

10. _____

The words below may prompt your recollection
of <u>activities</u> you are grateful for and why:

Reading / Studying	Teaching / Learning	Exercise / Yoga
Praying / Meditating	Biking / Swimming	Walking / Jogging
Writing / Creating	Building	Fixing / Repairing
Volunteering / Donating	Cooking / Cleaning	Helping / Assisting

Day 70

Day:_____ Date:____/____/_____

Today I am Grateful for…

1. _____

2. _____

3. _____

4. _____

5. _____

6. _____

7. _____

8. _____

9. _____

10. _____

A quality I like about myself is…

_____

*because*_____

_____

_____

"At the age of 18, I made up my mind to never have another bad day in my life. I dove into an endless sea of gratitude from which I've never emerged."

~ Patch Adams

Pause & Review

As I review my entries of the past 10 days, these are the experiences of Gratitude that were most meaningful to me and why...

1. _____

   _____

2. _____

   _____

3. _____

   _____

4. _____

   _____

Express Your Gratitude

As I reflect on my life, including recent events,
these are people I will express Gratitude to right away:

Name	Reason to Thank Them	What I Will Do

Schedule and follow through on your actions to thank them
(e.g., conversation, phone call, text, email, card, gift, meal, etc.).
They will appreciate being appreciated!

Draw Someone or Something You're Grateful For!

Personal Check-In

*How is this daily practice of Gratitude
improving my life, circumstances, and relationships?
And how do I feel about these developments?*

_____

_____

_____

_____

_____

_____

Have a Grateful Next 10 days!

Day 71

Today I am Grateful for…

1. _____

2. _____

3. _____

4. _____

5. _____

6. _____

7. _____

8. _____

9. _____

10. _____

The words below may prompt your recollection
of who and what you are grateful for and why:

Spouse / Partner	Parent / Child / Sibling	Teacher / Friend
Colleague / Co-Worker	Conversation	Meeting / Gathering
Spirituality / Faith / Belief	Reading / Study / Class	Skill / Talent / Ability
Event / Movie / Meal	Challenge / Problem	Opportunity
Accomplishment	Insight / Discovery	Project / Work
Lesson Learned	Help / Assistance	Purchase / Sale
Inspiration	Compliment	Breakthrough
Trip / Outing	Gift / Benefit	Pet / Nature

Day 72

Day:_____ Date:_____/_____/_____

Today I am Grateful for…

1. _____

2. _____

3. _____

4. _____

5. _____

6. _____

7. _____

8. _____

9. _____

10. _____

Daily Reflection:
"I am grateful for these people and experiences in my life!
They are helping me grow into a stronger, better,
and more successful person! Thank you!"

"Let gratitude be the pillow upon which you kneel to say
your nightly prayer. And let faith be the bridge
to overcome evil and welcome good."

~ Maya Angelou

Day 73

Day:_____ Date:_____/_____/_____

Today I am Grateful for…

1. _____

2. _____

3. _____

4. _____

5. _____

6. _____

7. _____

8. _____

9. _____

10. _____

The words below may prompt your recollection
of <u>who</u> you are grateful for and why:

Spouse	Partner	Parent
Child	Sibling	Grandparent
Relative	Teacher / Pastor	Mentor / Coach
Friend	Colleague	Co-Worker
Customer	Neighbor	Stranger

Day 74

Day:_____ Date:_____/_____/_____

Today I am Grateful for...

1. _____

2. _____

3. _____

4. _____

5. _____

6. _____

7. _____

8. _____

9. _____

10. _____

A key to success I've discovered in life is...

_____

_____

*It has helped me*_____

_____

_____

*"We often take for granted the very things
that most deserve our gratitude."*

~ Cynthia Ozick

Day 75

Day:_____ Date:____/____/_____

Today I am Grateful for...

1. _____

2. _____

3. _____

4. _____

5. _____

6. _____

7. _____

8. _____

9. _____

10. _____

The words below may prompt your recollection
of __what__ you are grateful for and why:

Spirituality / Faith / Belief	Help / Assistance	Skill / Talent / Ability
Movie / Show	Meal / Food	Housing / Shelter
Purchase / Sale	Letter / Message	Book / Article
Pet	Nature	Class / Course
Art / Music	Job / Career	Health

Day 76

Day:_____ Date:____/____/_____

Today I am Grateful for…

1. _____

2. _____

3. _____

4. _____

5. _____

6. _____

7. _____

8. _____

9. _____

10. _____

If I had wings and could fly anywhere, I'd fly to these places…

_____

_____

*I'd go there because*_____

_____

_____

"Happiness doesn't depend on any external conditions,
it is governed by our mental attitude."

~ Dale Carnegie

Day 77

Day:_____ Date:____/____/_____

Today I am Grateful for...

1. _____
2. _____
3. _____
4. _____
5. _____
6. _____
7. _____
8. _____
9. _____
10. _____

The words below may prompt your recollection
of <u>experiences</u> you are grateful for and why:

Conversation	Meeting / Gathering	Trip / Outing
Accomplishment	Insight / Discovery	Work Project
Challenge / Problem	Lesson Learned	Opportunity
Inspiration	Compliment	Breakthrough
Giving a Gift	Receiving a Gift	Benefit Received

Day 78

Day:_____ Date:_____/_____/_____

Today I am Grateful for...

1. _____

2. _____

3. _____

4. _____

5. _____

6. _____

7. _____

8. _____

9. _____

10. _____

My favorite holiday is...

_____

*because*_____

_____

_____

_____

*"Gratitude is the single most important ingredient
to living a successful and fulfilled life."*

~ Jack Canfield

Day 79

Day:_____ Date:_____/_____/_____

Today I am Grateful for…

1. _____

2. _____

3. _____

4. _____

5. _____

6. _____

7. _____

8. _____

9. _____

10. _____

The words below may prompt your recollection
of <u>activities</u> you are grateful for and why:

Reading / Studying	Teaching / Learning	Exercise / Yoga
Praying / Meditating	Biking / Swimming	Walking / Jogging
Writing / Creating	Building	Fixing / Repairing
Volunteering / Donating	Cooking / Cleaning	Helping / Assisting

Day 80

Day:_____ Date:____/____/_____

Today I am Grateful for...

1. _____

2. _____

3. _____

4. _____

5. _____

6. _____

7. _____

8. _____

9. _____

10. _____

One of the best presents I ever received was...

_____

*I really appreciated it because*_____

_____

_____

_____

> *"When you give appreciation in order to get something it's manipulation and people can sense it. Appreciate genuinely."*
>
> *~ Marilyn Suttle*

Pause & Review

As I review my entries of the past 10 days, these are the experiences of Gratitude that were most meaningful to me and why...

1. _____

   _____

2. _____

   _____

3. _____

   _____

4. _____

   _____

Express Your Gratitude

*As I reflect on my life, including recent events,
these are people I will express Gratitude to right away:*

Name	Reason to Thank Them	What I Will Do

Schedule and follow through on your actions to thank them
(e.g., conversation, phone call, text, email, card, gift, meal, etc.).
They will appreciate being appreciated!

Draw Someone or Something You're Grateful For!

Personal Check-In

*How is this daily practice of Gratitude
improving my life, circumstances, and relationships?
And how do I feel about these developments?*

_____

_____

_____

_____

_____

_____

Have a Grateful Next 10 days!

Day 81

Day:_____ Date:____/____/_____

Today I am Grateful for...

1. _____

2. _____

3. _____

4. _____

5. _____

6. _____

7. _____

8. _____

9. _____

10. _____

The words below may prompt your recollection
of who and what you are grateful for and why:

Spouse / Partner	Parent / Child / Sibling	Teacher / Friend
Colleague / Co-Worker	Conversation	Meeting / Gathering
Spirituality / Faith / Belief	Reading / Study / Class	Skill / Talent / Ability
Event / Movie / Meal	Challenge / Problem	Opportunity
Accomplishment	Insight / Discovery	Project / Work
Lesson Learned	Help / Assistance	Purchase / Sale
Inspiration	Compliment	Breakthrough
Trip / Outing	Gift / Benefit	Pet / Nature

Day 82

Day:_____ Date:_____/_____/_____

Today I am Grateful for...

1. _____

2. _____

3. _____

4. _____

5. _____

6. _____

7. _____

8. _____

9. _____

10. _____

A work of art that brings me joy is...

_____

_____

*What impresses me about it is*_____

_____

_____

> *"Gratitude is a powerful catalyst for happiness.*
> *It's the spark that lights a fire of joy in your soul."*
>
> *~ Amy Collette*

Day 83

Today I am Grateful for…

1. _____

2. _____

3. _____

4. _____

5. _____

6. _____

7. _____

8. _____

9. _____

10. _____

The words below may prompt your recollection of <u>who</u> you are grateful for and why:

Spouse	Partner	Parent
Child	Sibling	Grandparent
Relative	Teacher / Pastor	Mentor / Coach
Friend	Colleague	Co-Worker
Customer	Neighbor	Stranger

Day 84

Day:_____ Date:____/____/_____

Today I am Grateful for...

1. _____

2. _____

3. _____

4. _____

5. _____

6. _____

7. _____

8. _____

9. _____

10. _____

One thing I enjoyed about my work recently was...

_____

*because*_____

_____

_____

"Two kinds of gratitude:
The sudden kind we feel for what we take;
the larger kind we feel for what we give."

~ Edwin Arlington Robinson

Day 85

Day:_____ Date:_____/_____/_____

Today I am Grateful for...

1. _____

2. _____

3. _____

4. _____

5. _____

6. _____

7. _____

8. _____

9. _____

10. _____

The words below may prompt your recollection
of <u>what</u> you are grateful for and why:

Spirituality / Faith / Belief	Help / Assistance	Skill / Talent / Ability
Movie / Show	Meal / Food	Housing / Shelter
Purchase / Sale	Letter / Message	Book / Article
Pet	Nature	Class / Course
Art / Music	Job / Career	Health

Day 86

Day:_____ Date:____/____/_____

Today I am Grateful for…

1. _____

2. _____

3. _____

4. _____

5. _____

6. _____

7. _____

8. _____

9. _____

10. _____

I appreciate my dear friend (name): _____

*because*_____

_____

_____

_____

> *"We think we have to do something to be grateful or something has to be done in order for us to be grateful, when gratitude is a state of being."*
>
> *~ Ivanla Vanzant*

Day 87

Today I am Grateful for...

1. _____

2. _____

3. _____

4. _____

5. _____

6. _____

7. _____

8. _____

9. _____

10. _____

The words below may prompt your recollection
of <u>experiences</u> you are grateful for and why:

Conversation	Meeting / Gathering	Trip / Outing
Accomplishment	Insight / Discovery	Work Project
Challenge / Problem	Lesson Learned	Opportunity
Inspiration	Compliment	Breakthrough
Giving a Gift	Receiving a Gift	Benefit Received

Day 88

Day:_____ Date:_____/_____/_____

Today I am Grateful for...

1. _____

2. _____

3. _____

4. _____

5. _____

6. _____

7. _____

8. _____

9. _____

10. _____

A big mistake I made that I learned from was...

_____

*I learned*_____

_____

_____

"Being thankful is not always experienced as a natural state of existence, we must work at it, akin to a type of strength training for the heart."

~ Larissa Gomez

Day 89

Day:_____ Date:_____/_____/_____

Today I am Grateful for…

1. _____

2. _____

3. _____

4. _____

5. _____

6. _____

7. _____

8. _____

9. _____

10. _____

The words below may prompt your recollection
of <u>activities</u> you are grateful for and why:

Reading / Studying	Teaching / Learning	Exercise / Yoga
Praying / Meditating	Biking / Swimming	Walking / Jogging
Writing / Creating	Building	Fixing / Repairing
Volunteering / Donating	Cooking / Cleaning	Helping / Assisting

Day 90

Day:_____ Date:____/____/_____

Today I am Grateful for...

1. _____

2. _____

3. _____

4. _____

5. _____

6. _____

7. _____

8. _____

9. _____

10. _____

A success I achieved that I'm grateful for is...

_____

*I'm proud of it because*_____

_____

_____

> *"Gratitude bestows reverence, allowing us to encounter everyday epiphanies, those transcendent moments of awe that change forever how we experience life and the world."*
>
> *~ John Milton*

Pause & Review

As I review my entries of the past 10 days, these are the experiences of Gratitude that were most meaningful to me and why...

1. _____

    _____

2. _____

    _____

3. _____

    _____

4. _____

    _____

Express Your Gratitude

*As I reflect on my life, including recent events,
these are people I will express Gratitude to right away:*

Name	Reason to Thank Them	What I Will Do

Schedule and follow through on your actions to thank them
(e.g., conversation, phone call, text, email, card, gift, meal, etc.).
They will appreciate being appreciated!

Draw Someone or Something You're Grateful For!

Personal Check-In

*After these 90 days, how has this daily practice of Gratitude
improved my life, circumstances, and relationships?
And how do I feel about these developments?*

_____

_____

_____

_____

_____

_____

Ta-dah! You completed the 90 Days!

LETTER TO SELF

Dear _____,
Your Name

Congratulations!
You completed the 90-day Gratitude Journey!

You learned a lot during this time. You took big strides in developing a grateful heart and mind for everyone and everything that came your way.

Keep it going. Don't stop now! The past 90 days were a launch, a foundation. Continue to grow in gratitude each day going forward. You and everyone around you will benefit.

Again, great job in starting to build this habit of gratitude into your life!

I'm proud of you!

_____   _____
Your Name   Date

ENJOY A SUMMARY REVIEW

Go back and review the pages of your journal from the beginning to end to recall again who and what you are grateful for. Each page will remind you of key reflections you've had on this 90-day Gratitude Journey. They are your treasure and will remain within you and help power you forward in your ever-deepening, daily practice of gratitude.

GRATITUDE RESOURCES

What is Gratitude and Why Is It So Important?
by Courtney E. Ackerman, MSc.
https://positivepsychology.com/gratitude-appreciation/

Giving Thanks Can Make You Happier
https://www.health.harvard.edu/healthbeat/giving-thanks-can-make-you-happier

13 Ways Gratitude Will Significantly Improve Your Life
https://www.psychologytoday.com/us/blog/feeling-it/201406/13-ways-gratitude-will-significantly-improve-your-life

How Gratitude Changes You and Your Brain
https://greatergood.berkeley.edu/article/item/how_gratitude_changes_you_and_your_brain

Giving Thanks Can Keep Marriages Going
https://news.uga.edu/giving-thanks-can-keep-marriages-going/

28 Benefits of Gratitude & Most Significant Research Findings
https://positivepsychology.com/benefits-gratitude-research-questions/

7 Scientifically Proven Benefits Of Gratitude That Will Motivate You To Give Thanks Year-Round
https://www.forbes.com/sites/amymorin/2014/11/23/7-scientifically-proven-benefits-of-gratitude-that-will-motivate-you-to-give-thanks-year-round/

Find more Gratitude Resources by typing these phrases at your favorite online search engine:
- *Gratitude Tips*
- *Gratitude Quotes*
- *Gratitude Practice*
- *Gratitude Posters*
- *Gratitude Lessons*
- *Gratitude Exercises and Activities*

Please Post a Review at Amazon!

Thank you for getting this 90-Day Gratitude Journal.
I hope you benefited greatly from using it to help develop
your personal attitude of gratitude.

I would really appreciate your feedback.

Please go to the journal at Amazon.com,
scroll down the home page, and click on
"Write a customer review"
and let me know what you thought of the book
and what you may have gained from it.

Keep It Going!

Order A Fresh Copy of the Journal Today!
Start a new 90-Day cycle to keep your
routine of gratitude writing going
and get stronger and stronger at it.

Also, consider giving it as a Gift
to a family member or friend.

Order at Amazon.com
or click on "Get the Journal" at
bentoleal.com
which will take you directly
to the journal at Amazon.

No matter what, continue the practice of having
a grateful heart and mind each day for all
the people and experiences in your life.
You'll be the better for it!

Want To Build Relationships
You Will Be Grateful For?

Get this book!
I wrote it to help you grow your communication skills
to experience greater joy, satisfaction, and gratitude
in ALL your relationships!

Available in eBook, Paperback, and Audiobook
at Amazon.com
or click on "Get the Book" at
bentoleal.com

May you live today and always
in the spirit of gratitude!

Made in the USA
Monee, IL
20 June 2023

36413884R00068